Seven Days with God

David Meador

Illustrated by Brianna Showalter

Seven Days with God
First Edition Trade Book, 2018
Copyright © 2018 by David Meador

All rights reserved. No part of this publication may be reproduced, stored in a retrieval system, or transmitted in any form by any means—electronic, mechanical, photocopy, recording, or otherwise—except for brief quotations in critical reviews or articles, without the prior permission of the author, except as provided by U.S. copyright law.

Scripture quotations marked TLB are taken from The Living Bible copyright © 1971 by Tyndale House Foundation. Used by permission of Tyndale House Publishers Inc., Carol Stream, Illinois 60188. All rights reserved. The Living Bible, TLB, and the The Living Bible logo are registered trademarks of Tyndale House Publishers.

Scripture quotations marked ICB are taken from The Holy Bible, International Children's Bible® Copyright© 1986, 1988, 1999, 2015 by Tommy Nelson™, a division of Thomas Nelson. Thomas Nelson is a registered trademark of HarperCollins Christian Publishing, Inc.

Scripture quotations marked VOICE are taken from The Voice™. Copyright © 2012 by Ecclesia Bible Society. Used by permission. All rights reserved.

Scripture quotations marked The Message are taken from THE MESSAGE, copyright © 1993, 1994, 1995, 1996, 2000, 2001, 2002 by Eugene H. Peterson. Used by permission of NavPress. All rights reserved. Represented by Tyndale House Publishers, Inc.

Scripture quotations marked ISV are taken from the Holy Bible: International Standard Version®. Copyright © 1996-forever by The ISV Foundation. ALL RIGHTS RESERVED INTERNATIONALLY. Used by permission.

ISBN: 978-1-7329092-0-5

To order additional books:
www.amazon.com
www.sevendayswithgod.com

Editorial and Book Production: Inspira Literary Solutions, Gig Harbor, WA
Book Design: Brianna Showalter, Ruston, WA
Illustrations: Brianna Showalter, Ruston, WA

For my daughter, Leila

Seven Days with God was a vision I had in the first few weeks after finding out my wife and I were expecting our first child. What I wanted more than anything was for my daughter to know the peace, contentment, and fun that come with a genuine relationship with God.

The pictures and message in this book are for the kids, but the concepts are true and inviting no matter how old you are. For each day of the week, there is a truth to explore (and you can go as in depth as you'd like). I believe that investigating each day's truth—even for as little as a minute—would make a significant difference in each of our lives.

I hope you'll use this book to connect with the children in your life, and to connect them to the facts that God loves them, they are special, and they are never alone.

David Meador

Monday is a day to remember God loves you so much.

Did you know God is your biggest fan?

When God sees you, He smiles, because He loves you so much!

His love for you is so big; it is bigger than the stars and the moon.

He will never stop loving you, no matter what.

Even on your bad days, remember that God loves you.

Words to live by:

"And so we know the love that God has for us, and we trust that love. God is love."
1 John 4:16 (ICB)

"But you, Lord, are a compassionate God, merciful and patient, with unending gracious love and faithfulness."
Psalm 86:15 (ISV)

"...Nothing else in the whole world will ever be able to separate us from the love of God that is in Christ Jesus our Lord."
Romans 8:39b (ICB)

Prayer:

Dear God,

It makes me happy to know how much You love me. I love You, too, God. And I know You love me all the time, no matter what. If I am good or bad, happy or sad, Your love for me does not change. Thank you, God.

Amen.

Things to talk about:

1. What is something you love very much?

2. Whom is someone you love?

3. Who loves you?

4. How does it make you feel to know you are loved by God?

Tuesday is a day to remember God made you special.

God made you so special! There is no one else like you!
God designed and created you to do something only you can do.

Do you like to sing? Run fast? Draw pictures? Take care of others?
God gave you those talents and abilities, and they make you, YOU!

He is very happy with the special person He created.
You are a gift to this earth!

Words to live by:

"Before I made you…I chose you. Before you were born, I set you apart for a special work."
Jeremiah 1:5 (ICB)

"God has given each of you some special abilities; be sure to use them to help each other."
1 Peter 4:10 (TLB)

"For You shaped me, inside and out. You knitted me together long before I took my first breath."
Psalm 139:13-14 (VOICE)

Prayer:

Dear God,

Thank You for creating me. I know You gave me special talents and unique gifts. Please help me to see those gifts and use them. I know You have a great plan for my life, and I am excited to find out what it is. I love You very much.

Amen.

Things to talk about:

1. Who made you?

2. What is something unique or special about you?

3. What is your favorite thing about yourself?

4. What is something special about the people you love?

Wednesday is a day to remember to talk with God.

Did you know God loves it when you talk with Him?

He is a great listener, and wants to hear all about your day.
Tell Him what great things happened to you or what things made you sad today.
Or, tell God what you love about Him.

You can talk to God anywhere—in your bed, in the car, or even at the park!
God loves spending time with you.

Words to live by:

"Depend on the Lord and his strength. Always go to him for help."
1 Chronicles 16:11 (ICB)

"In those days when you pray, I will listen."
Jeremiah 29:12 (TLB)

"Give all your worries to him, because he cares for you."
1 Peter 5:7 (ICB)

Prayer:

Dear God,
I feel so lucky that I get to speak with You any time I want. You are my heavenly Father and I know I can always share my heart with You. Whether I'm happy or sad, angry or afraid, You are here to listen. It makes me feel good to know I always have someone to talk to. Thank You, God.
Amen.

Things to talk about:

1. What are some things you want to tell God?

2. How is your heart feeling today? God wants to know. Are you happy? Sad? Mad?

3. What was your favorite part of your day today? Let's tell God about it.

4. What was hard for you today? We can tell God about that, too.

Thursday is a day to remember to love others.

One of the best things you can ever do is help others.

Whether its sharing a toy, or helping a friend who falls down,
or just offering an encouraging word to a friend having a bad day,
God loves it when we help others. And, the neat thing is,
it feels really good to do something kind for someone.
Jesus was really good at helping others.

Words to live by:

"If someone asks you for something, give it to him. If someone wants to borrow something from you, do not turn away."
Matthew 5:42 (VOICE)

"Help each other in troubles and problems. This is the kind of law Christ asks us to obey."
Galations 6:2 (NLV)

"...Love each other. You must love each other as I have loved you..."
John 13:34 (ICB)

"...love your neighbor as you love yourself." Matthew 22:39, ICB
Matthew 22:39 (ICB)

Prayer:

Dear God,
Thank You for being such a helpful and loving God to me. I want to be helpful and loving to the people around me, too. Please help me look for ways to love my family, friends, neighbors, and others living in my community. I know that when I am loving others, I am also loving You.
Amen.

Things to talk about:

1. Who helped you today? What did they help you do?

2. How does it make you feel when other people show kindness to you?

3. Who is someone you could help or show kindness to this week?

4. What is your favorite way to help/love others?

Friday is a day to remember that you are never alone.

Did you know that God is with you everywhere you go?

No matter where you are, or what is happening around you,
God is with you and Jesus is your friend. You are never alone.
God made you, He loves you, and He is always there for you.

Words to live by:

"…don't be afraid. The Lord your God is with you everywhere you go."
Joshua 1:9 (ICB)

"Let the little children come to Me; do not get in their way. For the kingdom of heaven belongs to children like these."
Matthew 19:14 (VOICE)

"…I call you friends because I have made known to you everything I heard from the Father."
John 15:15 (ICB)

Prayer:

Dear God,
Thank You for being with me today and every day after. And thank You for Your son, Jesus. Please help me to remember You are always with me, and that I always have a friend in Jesus.
Amen.

Things to talk about:

1. Who is a friend that you spent some time with today?

2. What did you enjoy about being with that friend?

3. How does it make you feel to know that Jesus and God are there for you whenever you need them?

4. What are some ways that you can spend time with God?

Saturday is a day to remember that being thankful is the best way to be happy.

Saturday is a day to remember the good things in your life.

You may be thankful for a comfy bed, a best friend, or a furry pet.
And, you can always be thankful that God is right there by your side, no matter what!

On good days, and on bad days, too, it's important be grateful for all you have.

Words to live by:

"What a beautiful thing, God, to give thanks."
Psalm 92:1 (The Message)

"Thank the Lord because he is Good. His love continues forever."
1 Chronicles 16:34 (ICB)

"Let's come before Him with thanksgiving. Let's sing songs to Him."
Psalm 95:2 (ICB)

Prayer:

Dear Heavenly Father,
I am so thankful for You and for Jesus. I am thankful for my family, friends, good food (like pancakes!), books, and laughter. I know You have given me these great things and so much more, and my heart is very grateful. I love You.
Amen.

Things to talk about:

1. What is something that happened today that you are thankful for?

2. Whom are you thankful for?

3. What are some ways you can show God you are thankful?

Sunday is a day to remember to rest.

Sunday is a day to rest and spend time with the people you love.

God took time to rest after He created all of the land, sea, plants, animals, and people, and He wants us to take a day to rest, too. When we take a day to rest, it shows we trust Him to take care of us.

It's good for us to take a day to slow down, enjoy the people we love, and rest our bodies and hearts.

Words to live by:

"Come to me, all of you who are tired and have heavy loads. I will give you rest."
Matthew 11:28 (ICB)

"By the seventh day God finished the work he had been doing. So on the seventh day he rested from all his work."
Genesis 2:2 (ICB)

"Come with me. We will go to a quiet place to be alone. There we will get some rest."
Mark 6:31 (ICB)

Prayer:

Dear God,
Thank You for giving us a day of rest. Please show us how to use this day to slow down, remember You, rest our minds, and trust You. Help us feel Your peace in our hearts as we enjoy spending time with the people we love. We love you, God.
Amen.

Things to talk about:

1. Why do you think God wants us to remember to rest?

2. How do you feel when you don't take time to slow down and rest?

3. What are your favorite ways to spend quiet time and rest? (like reading a book, watching a movie, taking a nap, going for a nature walk with family, etc.)

www.sevendayswithgod.com